Animal Embroidery Workbook For Adult

Guide To Know About Embroidery Tool And Patterns

Copyright © 2020

All rights reserved.

DEDICATION

The author and publisher have provided this e-book to you for your personal use only. You may not make this e-book publicly available in any way. Copyright infringement is against the law. If you believe the copy of this e-book you are reading infringes on the author's copyright, please notify the publisher at: https://us.macmillan.com/piracy

Animal Embroidery Workbook For Adult

Contents

Embroidering With Sewing Threads 1

Embroidery Threads 6

Animal Embroidery Patterns 17

Embroidering With Sewing Threads

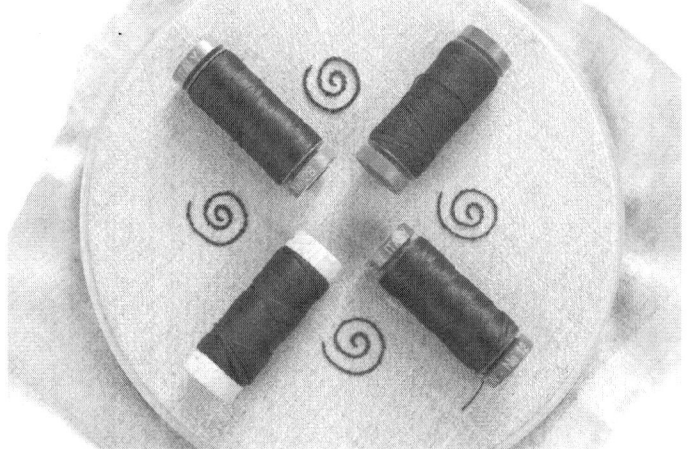

Have you ever looked at the racks of beautiful threads and wished they were actually spools of embroidery floss? We have, which made me wonder what would happen if we tried hand embroidery with thread designed for a sewing machine.

The very idea felt like breaking the rules, so if you're an embroidery purist this article may make you uncomfortable. And we understand.

Aurifil is an Italian thread company best known for their high-quality sewing threads. In recent years they added a line of embroidery floss called Aurifloss. We received a few spools of thread in the different weights and types they manufacture and thought this was a good opportunity to test out a new idea.

The short version of all of this is, you can use sewing threads for your hand stitching! The result and process are much like working with embroidery threads, and as with other threads, the different types have unique looks.

Take a look at these stitch samples then apply the idea to your own embroidery!

Stitching With Embroidery Floss

For the sake of comparison, let's start with a sample stitched with embroidery floss.

We often work with three strands, so that's what we did for this example. However, because this thread is a little thinner, you could very easily use all six strands for general embroidery.

As this is the most common type of thread for embroidery artists to work with, consider this the baseline with which to compare the other threads.

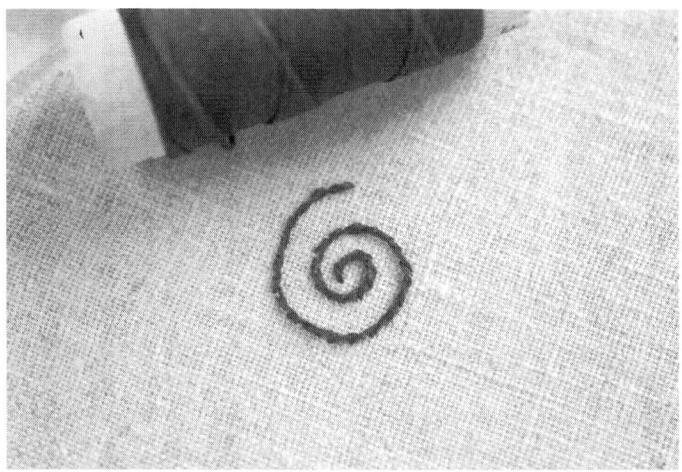

Stitching With 28wt Sewing Thread

Sewing threads come in different weights, which often are related to their intended use. The weights are also used simply to create a different look in the stitching. A larger number indicates a thinner thread and the basic thread we typically think of would be 40wt or 50wt.

For our testing, we went for a slightly thicker thread: 28wt, which is recommended for machine embroidery Just feeling it, we thought this might be similar to a single strand of embroidery floss, but it's actually a little thicker. Maybe even a lot thicker, which tells me that using finer thread would be a good option too.

To stitch the sample, we cut off three strands of the 28wt thread, held them together and threaded our embroidery needle.

Of course, all threads are different, but what made this really shine was that it has a smoothness and sheen to it that most floss lacks. The look is similar to perle cotton but less chunky. We'll be using this thread again.

Stitching with 12wt Sewing Thread

Switching to an even thicker thread, next we embroidered with 12wt thread, designed for decorative sewing/quilting. Embroidery is a form of decorative sewing, so it was no surprise that this one worked well.

The weight of this could be compared to fine weight perle cotton. Sulky makes a product in the same weight, and they compare this to two strands of floss.

We embroidered the sample with just one strand or piece of 12wt. Similar to the thinner thread, this has a beautiful shine to it and was easy to work with.

This is clearly a good choice for embroidery.

Stitching With Wool Sewing Thread

Finally, another product that Aurifil makes is a wool thread. It's recommended for machine applique and quilting, but also for some hand work. And it truly is ideal.

As soon as we saw this, we thought about crewel work and wondered how it might compare to the wool threads designed for that type of embroidery. While it's finer than most of the crewel threads and handspun wool floss we've encountered, it would definitely work.

Again, we worked this example with just one strand. The stitching is soft and a little fuzzy, just as you would expect wool to be.

We also tried using this for some fill stitching, and the result was beautiful.

Conclusion

Don't be afraid to try a thread that looks interesting to you just because it's not designed for embroidery. It's okay to stitch outside the skein!

Experiment on your own and then try combining a few different kinds of threads in a single piece. The variety of weights and textures, even if they are all the same color, will add a new dimension to your embroidery.

Embroidery Threads

Threads for embroidery are available in a wide range of fibers, colors, types, and weights. Your choice of threads will depend on the type of fabric used, the fabric thread count, and the type of embroidery you are stitching.

There are very few hard-fast rules when it comes to selecting the embroidery thread. Use the type of thread or weight that looks best or has the effect you want to achieve in your project. Experimentation is often the best indicator of whether or not a thread will give you the desired look.

Embroidery Floss

Embroidery floss is easy to find and comes in a huge range of colors. The six individual plies of embroidery floss can be separated, so you can use the thickness that is best suited for your project by combining plies. Visit the tutorial to learn how to separate floss without tangling.

Always use threads from the same manufacturer in an embroidery project that uses floss, as the finish on the threads can vary from shiny to matte.

Pearl Cotton

Pearl Cotton is a single-ply embroidery thread with a lustrous, pearly finish due to a process called mercerization.

Pearl cotton is available in a variety of weights or thicknesses, and depending on the weight can be available in a twisted skein or a ball.

A wide range of colors is available for size 5 pearl cotton, with a lesser variety for size 8. Other sizes have a limited color selection.

When selecting pearl cotton, remember that the larger the number, the finer the thread.

Silk Threads

Silk threads have a soft hand and are a joy to stitch with—but these threads can be expensive.

Silk threads for embroidery are available in embroidery floss, pearl, and other weights, as well as fine ribbon. Use silk thread as you would any other thread.

Metallic Threads

Animal Embroidery Workbook For Adult

Use metallic threads to add glitz and glamor to your embroidery projects.

Narrow weights of metallic thread can be stitched directly onto the fabric, while thicker or wired varieties should be couched to the surface of the project.

Weights for metallic threads can be very fine and whispy to very thick and somewhat stiff. Metallics are also available in floss, single-ply or pearl cotton varieties.

Colors include gold, silver, and platinum as well as copper and antique or aged versions.

Satin and Rayon Threads

Satin and rayon threads are synthetic threads that are shiny like satin. These threads are usually packaged as floss that can be separated or single-ply threads such as braids, narrow ribbon, or holographic ribbon.

Synthetics can be unruly to stitch with, so keep some thread conditioner handy when using these types of threads.

Overdyed Threads

Overdyed threads feature more than one color in a single strand and can be hand-dyed or mass-produced. Weights can vary, and overdyed threads are often produced in cotton or silk embroidery floss and varying weights of pearl cotton.

Overdyed threads are not to be confused with variegated thread or floss, which features varying shades of a single color.

Wool Threads

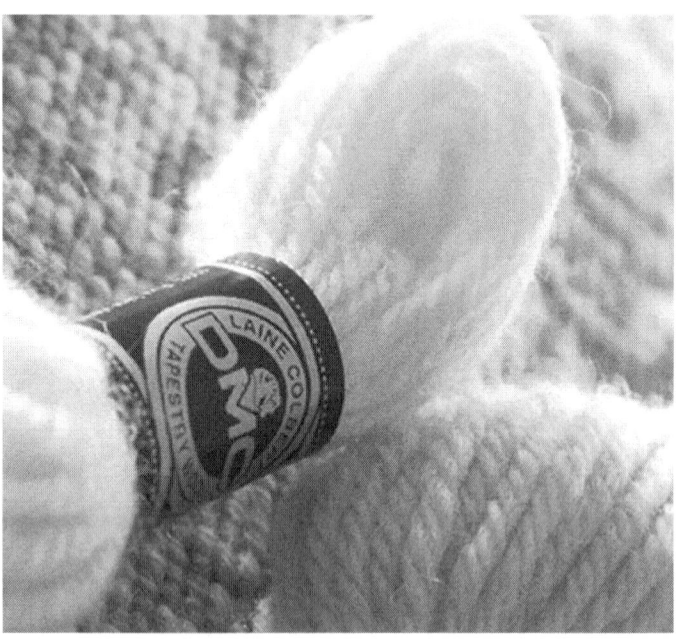

Wool threads come in a variety of weights, including very fine crewel wool, divisible Persian wool, and tapestry wool (most commonly used in needlepoint).

Ribbon

Animal Embroidery Workbook For Adult

Many different types of ribbon can be used for embroidery. These ribbons can be silk, cotton, or synthetic and are available in varying widths, from a narrow 1/8 inch to 1/2 inch or larger.

This thread is used in ribbon embroidery, utilizing a variety of surface embroidery stitches, or it can be used as a decorative accent with other types of embroidery.

Floche

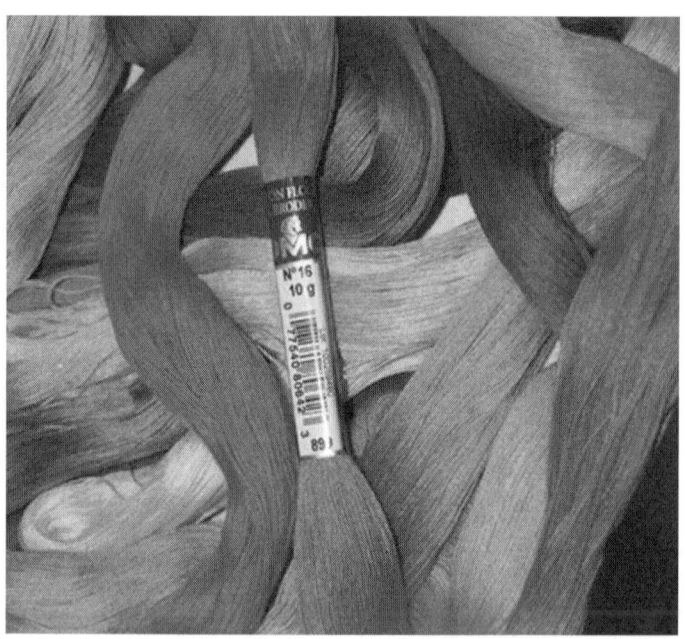

Floche is a size 16 mercerized, single-strand embroidery thread made from long-staple Egyptian cotton. This lustrous thread has a soft, luxurious hand and is most commonly used in whitework, cutwork, openwork, and needle painting.

Use a laying tool when stitching using multiple strands of floche to keep the stitches smooth and even.

Novelty Threads

Novelty threads encompass a wide range of styles, textures, materials, and supplies. They can be fuzzy, metallic, textured, leather, plastic, and more! Novelty threads are a lot of fun to stitch with and can add a fuzzy texture to a project including using a fuzzy thread for hair or beards and other special effects.

These types of threads can be difficult to work with, so be sure to choose an appropriate, often simple embroidery stitch. Otherwise, you could be fighting a losing battle with the thread.

Wired Threads

Wired threads are not normally used for stitching, but are instead stitched to the surface of a finished design to add texture, dimension, and detail to a project.

These threads can be bent, twisted, and curled and hold their shape due to the hidden interior wire.

Animal Embroidery Patterns

Animal Embroidery Workbook For Adult

Animal Embroidery Workbook For Adult

Animal Embroidery Workbook For Adult

Animal Embroidery Workbook For Adult

Animal Embroidery Workbook For Adult

Animal Embroidery Workbook For Adult

Animal Embroidery Workbook For Adult

Animal Embroidery Workbook For Adult

Animal Embroidery Workbook For Adult

Animal Embroidery Workbook For Adult

Animal Embroidery Workbook For Adult

Animal Embroidery Workbook For Adult

Animal Embroidery Workbook For Adult

Animal Embroidery Workbook For Adult

Animal Embroidery Workbook For Adult

Animal Embroidery Workbook For Adult

Animal Embroidery Workbook For Adult

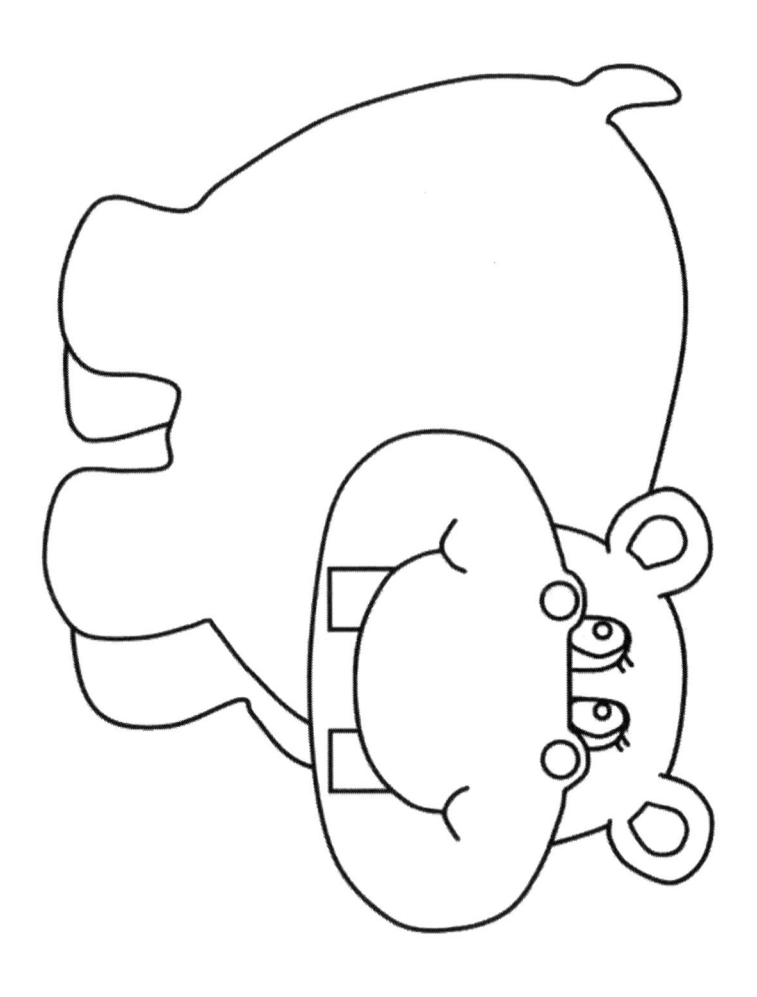